COVENANT • BIBLE • STUDIES

Jeremiah

Thomas A. Kinzie

faithQuest® ♦ Brethren Press®

Covenant Bible Studies Series

Unless otherwise noted, scripture quotations are from the New Revised Standard Version of the Bible, copyrighted 1989 by the National Council of Churches of Christ in the USA, Division of Education and Ministry.

Cover photo: D. Jeanene Tiner

03   02   01   00   99   5   4   3   2   1

Library of Congress Catalog Card No. 98-074587

Manufactured in the United States of America

Contents

Foreword

The Covenant Bible Studies Series was first developed for a denominational program in the Church of the Brethren and the Christian Church (Disciples of Christ). This program, called People of the Covenant, was founded on the concept of relational Bible study and has been adopted by several other denominations and small groups who want to study the Bible in a community rather than alone.

Relational Bible study is marked by certain characteristics, some of which differ from other types of Bible study. For one, it is intended for small groups of people who can meet face-to-face on a regular basis and share frankly with an intimate group. It is important to remember that relational Bible study is anchored in covenantal history. God covenanted with people in Old Testament history, established a new covenant in Jesus Christ, and covenants with the church today.

Relational Bible study takes seriously a corporate faith. As each person contributes to study, prayer, and work, the group becomes the real body of Christ. Each one's contribution is needed and important. "For just as the body is one and has many members, and all the members of the body, though many, are one body, so it is with Christ. . . . Now you are the body of Christ and individually members of it" (1 Cor. 12:12,17).

Relational Bible study helps both individuals and the group to claim the promise of the Spirit and the working of the Spirit. As one person testified, "In our commitment to one another and in our sharing, something happened. . . . We were woven together in love by the Master Weaver. It is something that can happen only when two or three or seven are gathered in God's name and we know the promise of God's presence in our lives."

For people who choose to use this study in a small group, the following guidelines will help create an atmosphere in which support will grow and faith will deepen.

1. As a small group of learners, we gather around God's word to discern its meaning for today.
2. The words, stories, and admonitions we find in scripture come alive for today, challenging and renewing us.
3. All people are learners and all are leaders.
4. Each person will contribute to the study, sharing the meaning found in the scripture and helping to bring meaning to others.
5. We recognize each other's vulnerability as we share out of our own experience, and in sharing we learn to trust others and to be trustworthy.

Additional suggestions for study and group-building are provided in the "Sharing and Prayer" section. They are intended for use in the hour preceding the Bible study to foster intimacy in the covenant group and relate personal sharing to the Bible study topic.

Welcome to this study. As you search the scriptures, may you also search yourself. May God's voice and guidance and the love and encouragement of brothers and sisters in Christ challenge you to live more fully the abundant life God promises.

Resources for This Study

Achtemeier, Elizabeth. *Jeremiah*. John Knox Press, 1987.

Boadt, Lawrence. *Jeremiah 1–25*. Michael Glazier, 1982.

Brueggemann, Walter. *The Hopeful Imagination*. Fortress Press, 1986.

Martens, Elmer A. and Howard H. Charles, eds. *Jeremiah* (Believers Church Bible Commentary). Herald Press, 1986.

Preface

One of the evangelists said, "You will know the truth, and the truth will make you free" (John 8:32), but somebody else may have been more accurate in saying "You will know the truth and the truth will make you sick." Is it any wonder that Jeremiah withered at the call to be a prophet, one who speaks God's truth? Nobody much likes hearing the truth about themselves and nobody much likes to have to tell it.

We have derogatory names for truth-tellers in our society. Environmentalists are called "tree huggers," antiwar advocates are called "ex-hippies," advocates for women's interests are called "feminazis," and people opposed to nuclear weapons are called "no nukes kooks." In one utterance, a little nickname discredits even a little common sense.

But even in the church, truth comes at a price. Years ago it was the practice among free churches (those without official government status) to never pay pastors, except as special needs arose. Eventually, however, pastors were getting professional degrees at seminaries and wanted to minister as a career. A salary allowed them to give full attention to the church, relieving them of having to farm or work for a wage somewhere else and care for the church as a second job. This new movement led to the fundamental question: If pastors are paid, will they be able to tell God's truth? Will they say what the people who pay them want to hear, or will they offend the people who pay them with the hard truth of the gospel?

Most pastors are paid these days. It's hard to say whether it's possible for them to tell the whole truth from the pulpit. One thing is certain, however; we parishioners remain the same as in Jeremiah's day. We give our offering, and for it we'd like to hear an inspiring word instead of being indicted every week. In many ways we have settled for small comforts when we could know the supreme feeling of being reconciled to God. Some sort of exile will come to us just as it came eventually to the Israelites. Then, though we didn't choose it, we'll know that the truth can set us free.

—Julie Garber

1

Called to Ministry
Jeremiah 1:1-19

*How does a person experience God's call? Jeremiah
tells how God's call to be a messenger came to him
and how he answered that call.*

Personal Preparation

1. What accommodations have you made in your faith for
   the culture you live in?
2. Do you feel you have a calling? What is it? How have
   you embraced or resisted your calling?
3. To what extent does your calling come from a gift you
   perceive in yourself, and to what extent does your calling come from God? If you don't do what God calls you
   to do, what would you like to do?
4. Does your calling as a peacemaker, counselor, musician,
   pastor, or teacher, for example, ever put you at odds with
   others? In what way?

Understanding

The Book of Jeremiah is far from easy to read. There was no one
author who sat at a desk and wrote Jeremiah with a clear beginning, middle, and end. Jeremiah was put together over a long
period of time, using a variety of sources, with the result that
sometimes Jeremiah does not make any chronological sense;
speeches are repeated or placed with the wrong event or seem to
be simply stuck in the text without regard to context.

Even though Jeremiah is a complex and sometimes confusing book to read, it is a rich source for reflection on what it means to be called to faithfulness as a person and as a people of God. In Jeremiah we see a person confronted both by God and by the historical-political situation of his time. It is in the interplay of these two confrontations that Jeremiah's and Israel's test of faithfulness come alive. God calls a person to ministry in and for a real time and place. Neither our lives nor Jeremiah's life is in a vacuum. Who we are, who Jeremiah was, are at least partially the result of what is happening around us. For many in my generation it would be impossible to talk about our lives without saying "Vietnam." For Jeremiah the words would have been "Assyria" and "Babylon."

By the time Jeremiah received his call to ministry, the Assyrian Empire was already in decline. But for more than two centuries, Assyria was the superpower of ancient Near Eastern politics. The land we think of as Israel had for some time been divided into two lands—the Northern Kingdom, Israel, and the Southern Kingdom, Judah, with its capital, Jerusalem. Two hundred years before the birth of Jeremiah, Assyria had forced the Northern Kingdom to become a vassal state and make yearly payments of gold and other gifts. A hundred years later Assyria destroyed Israel's capital, Samaria, and at that point the Northern Kingdom came to an end.

What saved Jeremiah's homeland, Judah, from destruction? Judah's kings had entered into political arrangements with the Assyrians, and so Judah was saved, although struggles for religious and political independence continued.

Still, Judah was a vassal state, and along with political subservience came religious and cultural tolerance of things outside the demands of Yahweh to worship no other gods.

In the midst of this religious and political tumult, God called Jeremiah to be a prophet, to be one of God's messengers. A new king, Josiah, began to break free of Assyria's control. In matters of religion Josiah supported reform. The Jerusalem temple was to be cleansed from things that subverted the true faith. In matters of politics, the Assyrian empire was reeling from its own internal power struggles. Josiah shrewdly began to make Israel independent again. He was able to establish control over much of the territory that had belonged to the Northern Kingdom and reunite the lands. Empires rising and falling, religious issues, reform movements, questions about orthodoxy, issues of nationalism and self-determination: such was the heady environment in which God called Jeremiah to be a messenger for faithfulness.

It was an historic moment in the history of our country on that cold December evening in 1955 when a tired Rosa Parks refused to vacate her bus seat after a Montgomery, Alabama, bus driver ordered her to do so in order to make room for white riders. It was the right moment, a critical moment, what theologians call a *kairos* moment. A woman says no, and a black community begins to say that it has had enough. When the first organizational meetings were held to plan the Montgomery bus boycott, a little-known, young and new pastor in town was nominated to head the boycott effort. He was surprised by the nomination, not sure if he was the right person for the job, but he accepted it. His name was Martin Luther King, Jr.

Like Rosa Parks and Martin Luther King, Jr., Jeremiah's call came at a critical and historic moment in the life of his nation and his religion. God not only called Jeremiah, but God called him in the middle of turmoil and conflict. How did Jeremiah hear that call?

When I was very young, my parents took me to see a film biography of the famed pastor Peter Marshall. I don't remember very much about the film except that at some point in Peter Marshall's life he heard God call him. All I remember now is that the moment seems to have been surrounded with bolts of lightening and dramatic action. (I don't know if this is how the film actually went but it is how my young mind experienced it.) For a long time after that, I assumed that a call from God would have to be equally exciting, dramatic, and clear. I spent a lot of time being disappointed that it never happened to me. It was like driving down a highway and being intent upon seeing a particular road sign that would say what exit to take. Of course, if we spend all of our time looking for just one kind of sign, a lot of scenery goes by unnoticed.

God's call to Jeremiah is filled with an incredible intimacy. God says to Jeremiah, "Before I formed you in the womb I knew you for my own; before you were born I consecrated you, I appointed you a prophet to the nations" (Jer. 1:5 NEB). This "knowing" of Jeremiah is like that of a loving couple. God's call to Jeremiah is rooted in God's love for Jeremiah; God knows who Jeremiah is and that Jeremiah has the necessary qualities—the right person at the right time. God's call to Jeremiah is bound up in the events of the time and in this relationship between them.

It is quite possible that a call to ministry may, in fact, be like a dramatic encounter, a certain and sure sign that one's life is to move in a very specific and different direction. Yet, it seems that a call to service emerges, whether dramatically or not, out of this relational intimacy between a person and God. God knows us and we begin to know God's will for us.

In the Bible many calls to ministry are answered first with a negative. (See, for example, the call of Moses in Exodus 3–4.) Is there a reason for this? Perhaps this should not be seen so much as willful disobedience, but as part of that difficult journey to a new understanding of ourselves—just how we are God's children, just how God's love for us can be shown in our lives. In any event, Jeremiah's first response is hardly a fiery "yes." Only after Jeremiah is assured of God's continual presence does the consecration service for ministry begin; God touches Jeremiah's mouth, and there is now a "personal union between God and prophet, between the speaker and the message" (Boadt 10).

Discussion and Action

1. Read Jeremiah 1:4-10 as a prayer. Read it once, pause for silent reflection, and then read it again, slowly. God "knew" Jeremiah. As a form of faith sharing, discuss how you have been known by God or the ways you have felt yourself known by God.

2. Have you ever felt/heard/discovered God's call to ministry and service? How did that happen? How did you become aware of it?

3. Do you feel that you are on the edge of responding to a call to ministry and service but that something is holding you back? Why do you feel reluctant?
4. Some have said that church denominations today are experiencing a crisis in leadership. Discuss whether this means that the church has depended too much on private, individual experiences of God's call to ministry and neglected its corporate vision and responsibility.
5. Think of ways your Covenant group can encourage and enable church members to hear God's call to ministry and service.

2

Living Water or Cracked Cisterns
Jeremiah 2–6

The prophet uses the images of "living water" and "cracked cisterns" to speak of idolatry. What idols ("cracked cisterns") have we made for ourselves?

Personal Preparation

1. No matter how strong or weak your faith is, what in the gospel message makes you squirm?
2. Do an idol inventory in your home. What conveniences are you unwilling to live without? Think about whether you would ever be willing to reduce your income. Could you get along without a car? How do money and possessions distract our attention from God? Is there any way in which money and possessions direct our attention to God? How?
3. How do you practice repentance? For what?
4. Think about how you have changed over your lifetime. In what ways has the change been good? In what ways are you dissatisfied with the changes? What made you change in each case?

Understanding

After a particularly dire gospel reading, one filled with all sorts of warnings and somber words, the priest said the usual words, though this time with a certain coyness in his voice and his eyes rolling, "This is the *Good* News of the Lord." Those of us in the small chapel laughed, but a bit nervously. Something of that mood must strike us now as we read the message Jeremiah conveys from God to the people.

In the speeches found in Jeremiah 2–6, the prophet paints a picture that is sweeping in its insistence that Israel and Judah have utterly failed in keeping their part of the covenantal bargain. Jeremiah seems not to know, or at least not to care, that reformation of character is made easier by positive feedback, concentrating less on flaws and failure and more on possibility and potential. In other words, here the "good news" sounds suspiciously like bad news.

As we reflect on these sermons of Jeremiah, it is especially important that we note our own feelings and reactions to the various images he uses. Some are very strong and far from flattering. But, as biblical scholar Elizabeth Achtemeier points out, since Christians understand themselves as part of the new and expanded covenant, the issue of covenantal faithfulness is no mere historical curiosity aimed only at those ancient and long-since-gone kingdoms. We're meant to squirm too.

The issue of idolatry can seem foreign to us. After all, we are not pagan worshipers of idols and pseudo-gods. Very few of us have shrines to the moon in our yards. Yet, I am writing this in the middle of Christmas season, which seems to get longer every year. Already the crowds at the malls are crushing, and some parents are worrying about how they are going to pay for all of the presents they "have to" buy in order to insure that Johnnie and Susie have the kind of Christmas little ones are supposed to have. Recently, while driving through town, I saw one house where the residents evidently wanted to make sure that all of their bases were covered. A beautiful nativity scene had been erected on one half of the front yard. An equally large and impressive Santa, sled, and reindeer decorated the other half of the yard. Just what are we celebrating (worshiping) in our culture anyway?

Idolatry is, in fact, Jeremiah's chief complaint. His charge, made in the way one might make a court lawsuit, is that Israel and Judah have violated the covenantal relationship by worshiping other gods. In Jeremiah 2:1-3, God recalls the early days, the "honeymoon" of their relationship, before Judah followed after other gods. Idolatry is adultery, to carry the metaphor further.

In Jeremiah 2:4-13, God protests like a wronged lover that the love lavished upon Israel was a waste, for now Judah has forsaken their God. "For my people have committed two evils: they have forsaken me, the fountain of living water, and dug out cisterns for themselves, cracked cisterns that can hold no water" (Jer. 2:13). This is in sorry contrast to the days of "unfailing devotion" of a better time. Constancy in devotion, in worship and service of God our covenantal partner, is worthy in itself, for ebbing of intimacy with God will open us to the very real possibility of intimacy with lesser gods. Elizabeth Achtemeier puts it well, "We apparently cannot live in a devotional vacuum very long. If we desert God, we always give our devotion to something else" (*Jeremiah* 24). Here is an argument for the development of a disciplined prayer life, a life that lasts beyond the emotional highs and lows of an initial encounter, the romance stage.

Jeremiah 4:1-4 calls the people to repent. To follow Bonhoeffer's famous suggestion, repentance is not cheap. It will cost us something: first, it will mean acknowledging the errors of our ways, and secondly, it will mean turning anew to God, who is the source and center of covenantal existence. Neither is easy and neither is done once and for all. Something of confession, humility, and dependency upon God's renewing love is built into the structure of believing existence. For this reason the psalmist cries out, "Create in me a clean heart, O God, and renew a right spirit within me" (Ps. 51:11 Book of Common Prayer).

The central biblical understanding of heart refers to the inner life and character of a person, the source of attention, purpose, and the will. Thus, the heart is the governing center of personality, thought, action, and character. We get a flavor of this when we talk about a committed person as one who is wholeheartedly involved. David Steindl-Rast pushes this a bit more when he writes, "Whenever we speak of the heart, we mean the whole person. Only at heart are we whole. The heart stands for that center of our being where we are one with ourselves, one with others, one with God. [It] means to live fully" (*Gratefulness, the Heart of Prayer* 202).

So we see that change of heart is crucial to Jeremiah. It is the central change apart from which there is no other genuine change. We cannot reduce Jeremiah's plea to moralistic teachings or behavior modifications. It is more fundamental than that. A wholehearted way of life is being asked for, a return to the loyalty of the covenantal relationship. Thus, there is no easy forgiveness, no easy repentance. God demands, through Jeremiah, the turn, return of the heart. "Circumcise your hearts," Judah, and then you will know of God's unfailing love. God's longing for Judah is soaring in its intensity. "If you will but come back to me, says the LORD, if you will banish your loathsome idols from my sight, and stray no more, if you swear by the life of the LORD, in truth, in justice and uprightness, then shall the nations pray to be blessed like you and in you shall they boast" (Jer. 4:1-2 NEB).

Nevertheless, the people still refuse to return to God. Judah wants a quick fix, a solution without pain. "Everyone is greedy for unjust gain; and from prophet to priest, everyone deals falsely. They have treated the wound of my people carelessly, saying, 'Peace, peace,' when there is no peace" (6:13b-14). It is this false optimism, this unwillingness to see the disease of unfaithfulness for the deadly thing it really is, which finally undermines the people's health.

So, false prophecy, world views that do not acknowledge sinfulness, prevent a return to God. Finally, however, it is the "stubborn and rebellious heart" that is Israel's undoing. Still, in spite of the dire warnings, pleadings, longings, and personal anguish of Jeremiah, the alienation of Israel remains. The heart is not softened. This is the bitterness of sin. The wholeness for which God calls us into being is torn apart in the alienation of betrayal (to ourselves, to others, to God). Truly, at those moments the destruction seems already complete, the judgment already final.

Discussion and Action

1. What is your immediate response to these sermons of Jeremiah? How would you respond if you heard someone preach as directly as he did? Are there ways of speaking the truth that might be counter-productive?

2. What images in the text particularly struck you? List those on a blackboard/newsprint and discuss your reactions to them.

3. What does it mean to have a change of heart in relationship to God? Have you ever experienced a change that was so powerful that it went to the center of who you are?

4. Make a list of the idols that Christians worship today.

5. Repentance is not an easy matter. Discuss the place of repentance in the life of the individual and in the life of the church. In what ways does your congregation incorporate repentance in its worship? Are there ways in which you would like to see repentance included in your corporate worship experience?

6. Take turns naming one thing you would like to repent of. Report weekly to the group on your success in practicing the art of repentance.

7. In what ways are we already judged for our unfaithfulness today?

3

Preaching for Reform
Jeremiah 7:1-15; 26

Do we hide behind "false notions of religious secu-
rity" today, the way the people of Jeremiah's time hid
behind their belief that God would protect them no
matter what?

Personal Preparation

1. Read Jeremiah 7:1-15 aloud to yourself. What gives you
   hope in the world?
2. Why do you think it's more difficult to be faithful than to
   be unfaithful?
3. Is God's faithfulness to us a sure thing? How long do you
   think God will tolerate our unfaithfulness? What could
   finally cause God to abandon the people?
4. What happens when people in your congregation or
   community speak out, calling for real reform in the
   church or society?

Understanding

The justly famed anti-nuclear activist Dr. Helen Caldicott, co-
founder of Physicians for Social Responsibility, was sometimes
charged with offering a too pessimistic view of the nuclear arms
race. She often described the nuclear arms race between the su-
perpowers as the single most important medical issue of our time
and voiced concern that, if it was not stopped immediately, there

soon would be no way to slow the increasingly autonomous technological impetus for more destructive and sophisticated weaponry. Critics would ask her, Where is the hope in your message?

The issue here is whether doomsday warnings really serve their purpose. Can people learn and change when only being warned of the worst consequences? A friend described to me his sense of hopelessness when at a quit-smoking clinic a dentist related the development of some mouth and throat cancers even among those who had quit smoking ten years before. My friend's first response to such disheartening news was to reach for his cigarettes. Where was the good news? Why should he even try to quit?

Could similar questions be asked of Jeremiah? In later chapters Jeremiah offers words of hope (see especially chapters 30–32), but at this point Jeremiah's sermons sound pretty bleak. In words that are hauntingly appropriate to us living in the nuclear age, God says through Jeremiah that "the land shall become a waste," that "death shall be preferred to life," that "the corpses of this people will be food" for bird and beast. All of this is pretty grim stuff! So, we have to wonder why Jeremiah spoke as he did. Knowing how much Jeremiah loved his people, we can only guess at the internal cost Jeremiah's own words caused for himself.

In the very early part of Jeremiah's vocation as a messenger for God, King Josiah of Judah instituted a series of religious reforms. These reforms were based on the discovery in the Jerusalem temple of a book of laws, which scholars now believe to have been the central part of the Book of Deuteronomy. One account of that discovery is 2 Kings 22. Following the death of Josiah, the momentum of the reforms under new kings Jehoiakim and Zedekiah gave way. Certainly, Jeremiah's tone in the so-called temple sermons found in Jeremiah 7 (a shorter version appears in Jeremiah 26) is hardly one of the confident and hope-filled reformer. Rather, Jeremiah's sermon is a response to the fundamental failure of religious reformation and a denouncement of the apostasy of the religious community. The persistence of the people in the ways of injustice and idolatry, their refusal to listen to God's word through the prophets, and their failure to live by covenantal guidelines are not only marks of the failure of reform. It has become the sentence of judgment of the people on themselves, the bringing of a judgment in which God will allow the nation to be destroyed through the victory of Judah's enemies.

If you recall some of the famous sermons by Dr. Martin Luther King, you may remember his powerful use of repetition. Standing at the outer gate of the temple, perhaps on a feast day when people are milling about, Jeremiah starts like an effective street preacher and gets right to the central issue while he still has his listeners' attention. "You keep saying, 'This place is the temple of the LORD, the temple of the LORD, the temple of the LORD!' This catchword of yours is a lie; put no trust in it" (7:5 NEB). That's bound to get someone's attention!

At stake here, in Jeremiah's view, is the people's false notion of religious security. Judah has begun to understand their covenantal relationship with God as a relationship which can never be broken. "God will not abandon us" is no longer a message of spiritual consolation in times of brokenness, but it has become twisted into an illegitimate sense of spiritual self-righteousness and self-sufficiency. What has been forgotten by Judah is that the covenantal relationship is first of all a gift, a privilege that carries with it not only a sense of God's providential care, but also the concomitant responsibility in daily life of reflecting the faithfulness of the people to God's caring. In other words, there is a conditional aspect to our relationship with God.

Judah's attempt to have the privilege of covenantal relationship without the responsibility is summarized by Jeremiah in two ways. First, the people of Judah must amend their behavior toward those who have the least power in their society—foreigners, orphans, and widows. Because such lists are common in the scriptures, we need to look beyond the familiarity of the words. We can be sure that Jeremiah, standing at the gate of the temple, did not intend to address the so-called faithless and irreligious of his time. Rather, Jeremiah directs his message to those who are most consistent in their religious observances. His words might be paraphrased in contemporary language as "How can you claim to be religious if you show no concern for those who are the most marginalized among you?" That conditional aspect of the covenantal relationship shows itself in a faithfulness that recognizes the face of God among those whom our culture (including our religious culture) judges to be the least lovely. In the general North American context perhaps the following questions apply. Does our faith include the poor, the elderly, the retarded, minorities, AIDS victims? Do we include these people in our religious life? This challenge to broaden our understanding of covenantal faithfulness is the ongoing challenge of our religious life.

Secondly, Jeremiah judges the state of Judah's religious life by the code of the Decalogue (Ten Commandments—see Jeremiah 7:9). Those of us raised on the New Testament sometimes forget just how important the Decalogue was for the life of Israel. The commands and prohibitions of the Decalogue provided the Israelite community with boundary markers of obedience and peoplehood. They established the conditions by which the people entered into and remained in community. To live apart from those conditions was to strike at the borders of Israel's faith map. Jeremiah ends this part of the sermon with words that underline the personal nature of the religious crisis Judah faces: this temple, God's house, is now a den of robbers (Jer. 7:11). It is God who is affronted. It is God who is grieved. That Jesus quoted Jeremiah simply underscores for us the continued forcefulness of Jeremiah's concerns (see Mark 11:17).

If we turn for a brief look at chapter 26 of Jeremiah, we find a parallel, though shorter, version of this sermon. It can hardly be surprising that Jeremiah's prediction of the destruction of the Jerusalem temple was greeted with less than overwhelming joy. Again, we see Jesus prefigured in Jeremiah. And, in our own time, we know only too well that criticism of the accepted norm brings reprisals, even death, from those who feel most threatened. The name of Archbishop Oscar Romero, who was assassinated while celebrating mass in a San Salvador chapel in 1980, must certainly be remembered in this instance. As importantly, we also need to remember the hundreds of unknown martyrs in Central America who have been murdered because they believed that walking with God also requires us to walk with the poor.

Discussion and Action

1. Discuss the idea that Jeremiah criticizes the people for saying "This is the temple of the Lord," because it reflects a "false notion of religious security." Can you think of objects or ideas that offer Christians today a "false notion of religious security"?
2. In your opinion, how well does your family of faith open its doors to those in your community who are different, whose existence may even challenge your life and beliefs?
3. Is the Decalogue an important map for those within the Christian community? What are the boundary markers of your faith community?
4. If Jeremiah came today and stood at the door of your church building, what do you think his message would be for your congregation?

4

Covenant Talk
Jeremiah 11–12

Jeremiah criticizes the people for having failed their covenant relationship with God, but the prophet also experiences the certainty that God will not abandon them.

Personal Preparation

1. Read Jeremiah 11–12. If everything is within the power of God, why do you think God has "allowed" the world to be in the shape it's in?
2. What assurances do people of strong faith have that God will rescue them or help them in times of trouble?
3. To what extent are you motivated to be faithful out of fear of God's judgment, and to what extent are you motivated by God's love?
4. Practice confession like Jeremiah this week. Meditate frankly on what you would like to say to God about the state of the world, your part in it, how you would like to change, and how much confidence you have in God.

Understanding

Consider this argument about the relationship of the faith of the Old and New Testaments. Equality and justice are themes that carry importance in both the Old and New Testament traditions. In the Old Testament we encounter a God who deals in wrath and indignation toward those who no longer remember their covenantal obligations to live with others in ways that reflect God's demands for justice and equality. Far from being a distant God who treats covenant partners with regal indifference, this God is actively involved in just how Israel carries out its obligations. God rebukes those who have wandered away from the central aims of the covenant. God takes sides with those who have been oppressed by the powerful and the rich. God calls the people to return to God, to wake up to a religiously and socially responsible existence.

In this view of the God-people relationship, human beings give honor to God not only through religious acts of devotion but as importantly, in the way human beings treat each other and the gifts of life that have been given to them. Whenever human beings fail to act as good stewards of God's trust and relationship, they are reminded, often by the prophets, of God's deep disappointment and the judgment that is to come.

It is easy to see how this God can be trivialized into a God who seems only the stern and ever vigilant parent. This God becomes fearful because the people (children) are too immature to be trusted with the correct behavior; the children constantly have to be watched, reminded, cajoled, and disciplined before they are able to behave in the mature, adult way this parent-God expects of them. The role of covenantal law is to make sure that everyone remembers what kind of behavior is expected of them in the first place. God and God's law are external enforcers of behavior for people whose internal resources are simply not sufficient for self-motivation and regulation.

On the other hand, the revelation of Jesus is an attempt to reclaim the image of the caring God. Jesus reveals a new basis for behavior other than fear of being found out by God. This new basis for behavior no longer requires an occasional slap on the hand. Now, full and abundant existence is measured not simply by what one does, but by the motivation (love) with which one does it.

The new life in Christ is based upon the internalized authority of God's grace and love, the movement of the Spirit. In her book *Ordinary People as Monks and Mystics*, Marsha Sinetar writes:

"In other words, the New Testament asks that we become fully human, that we serve from love instead of from fear or a sense of obligation, that we demonstrate a type of love which asks for everything we have. It is in this kind of maturity, in this kind of personal development, that true stewardship is rooted" (57).

Although Jeremiah does have a vision of the internally realized covenant (Jer. 31:32), this particular passage offers a different vision. Most scholars agree that this passage resembles the language, style, and theology of the Deuteronomic writings (the Book of Deuteronomy and the so-called Deuteronomistic history found in the books from Joshua to 2 Kings). Here Jeremiah acts as a new Moses proclaiming God's law, judging the people's disobedience to the law, and finally announcing God's judgment on Israel for their failure to obey. The announcement is harsh, for God's rejection of Israel is complete, "I now bring on them disaster from which they cannot escape; though they cry to me for help I will not listen" (11:11 NEB).

From the standpoint of how the Book of Jeremiah was put together, this passage can be understood as a looking backward from the perspective of the exile at the destruction of Jerusalem and the fall of Judah. The central question for the faithful in a foreign land was, Why has God allowed this terrible thing to happen? The answer from Jeremiah 11:1-17 is very clear. God and the people had entered into an agreement, a covenant. God had given the land of milk and honey to the people on one condition: that they agree to obey God. Because the people failed to keep their part of the bargain, God took away their land. That is the view of covenant in this passage.

In Jeremiah 11:18–12:17, we come to the first of Jeremiah's great "confessions." As biblical poetry the confessions are exceptional sources of beauty and depth, yet they also reveal something of Jeremiah's inner turmoil and struggle. For me, the most interesting part of the confession occurs in 12:1-6. Although Jeremiah begins with a statement of trust in God, the prophet leads into the deeper issue of the treachery he has experienced: "Why do the wicked prosper and traitors live at ease?" (12:1b NEB). It is a question about the relationship between the suffering of the just and the seeming success of the unjust. Here, it is really a plea: "God, take care of me now." Jeremiah trusts that God's justice will be vindicated in some impersonal future, but what of this present moment in which there is his pain: "Can't your justice be accomplished a little more quickly, God?"

God's response to Jeremiah's petition of 12:1 comes in verses 5 and 6. It is not an answer that immediately satisfies, for it says that God's time and calculations are not ours. "Jeremiah, if you think things are bad now then you'd better learn to trust even more, because things are really going to get rotten in the future. Things will *not* soon be put right, but rather you must find those resources of strength that will carry you even in the darkness of the present moment." Faith is the certainty in the midst of uncertainty that God's good will and love will triumph ultimately. Somehow, we are to draw even closer to God precisely in those moments when God seems most distant.

Anyway, that is God's answer to Jeremiah. We, too, know something of the power of such an answer: in relational failures when a personal world has collapsed, in life-threatening illness or the death of a loved one when the security we had counted on gives way, in political violence when the simple worth of human life is ignored—when for a moment, for several moments, despair seems the only option. Yet, through faith another answer emerges. It is the joyous answer of God. "I shall never abandon you," says the Holy One of Israel.

Discussion and Action

1. To what extent are external authorities still needed in your journey of faith? What are some of these?
2. How have you experienced the presence of God even in those times of abandonment?
3. Can God both judge and console us? Are those ever the same?
4. Is it all right to complain to God? Should such complaints be a part of our worship together? Is it even possible to hate God?

5

God's Answers to Prayer
Jeremiah 14–15

*Jeremiah intercedes with God on behalf of the people
and struggles with his vocation as prophet. The prayers
of the prophet offer models for understanding our own
prayer relationships with God.*

Personal Preparation

1. Read Jeremiah 14–15. Be conscious this week of how you pray. Do you ask for things, "complain" to God, give thanks, confess your shortcomings and ask for pardon? When do you pray?
2. What do you personally hope to achieve by prayer?
3. When has God answered your prayers? Which prayers did God grant? Which prayers did God answer no?
4. When you pray for forgiveness on the behalf of others, do you include yourself as one who needs forgiveness? Why or why not?

Understanding

This session deals with three main passages of scripture: two lament-style pieces (Jer. 14:1-16 and 14:17–15:4) and a wrenching "confession" from Jeremiah (15:5-21). The laments are similar in style and form, so it is helpful to look at these passages side by side to further discuss their implications.

I. LAMENT OVER THE DROUGHT **II. LAMENT OVER DEFEAT AND FAMINE**

14:1-16		14:17–15:4
	a. Description	
14:2-6		14:17-18
	b. Prayer for mercy	
14:7-9		14:19-22
	c. Yahweh's rejection	
14:10-12		15:1-4
	d. Condemnation of false prophets	
14:13-16		

In the two prayers (14:7-9 and 14:19-22), Jeremiah intercedes for the people. Here Jeremiah is not only the voice of God to the people, but Jeremiah is also the voice of the people to God. Jeremiah is mediator between God and the wandering, sinful nation, a mediator who expresses the hopes and the struggles of a people now caught up in a desperate situation.

The depth and immediacy of these passages is not lessened by the fact that they utilize standard forms of temple liturgical piety. (There are many examples of communal lament psalms; see, for example, Psalm 74.) What is remarkable is that in Jeremiah the lament is spoken in the first person plural, "Though our sins testify against us, yet act, O LORD, for thy own name's sake" (14:7 NEB).

Jeremiah does not set himself up as being different from the people for whom he is speaking. Jeremiah is intimately bound up in the plight of the nation. There is no easy "over againstness," no self-righteousness that accuses and condemns but is itself no longer involved in the struggle. Here, the "I" and "we" are interchangeable. Does that voice in Jeremiah tell us something about the authentic prophetic voice? Is it not a voice which, while pleading, cajoling, demanding, is still a voice that recognizes with empathy the perilous and costly path that leads to a new way of being in the world?

The voice of the often angry prophet is now seen as the voice of one who intercedes. The denouncer becomes the intercessor, "Thou art in our midst, O LORD, and thou hast named us thine; do not forsake us" (14:9b NEB). In Jeremiah's case it seems unlikely that this was merely a formal religious activity carried out in the temple; his alienation from the religious authorities was too profound for that.

How often are our prayers for others performed only as a kind of religious duty? How often are our prayers for peace and justice just something that is supposed to take place in a good religious service, something that shows we care for others? Do we expect our prayers to be heard by God, or, are they mouthed with little real hope in us?

No doubt some of the power of intercessory prayer has to do with the immediacy of that for which we are praying. A close friend or a relative is struggling with a life-threatening illness, a painful disruption in his or her personal life, or a sense of failure that casts a pall over his or her emotional well-being. In such situations our prayers for that person have depth and power; they are genuine cries for help and mercy to the One whose compassion is sorely needed. I have often wondered what the power of our prayers for peace and justice would be if we would pray for those with the same conviction that we pray for Uncle Joe's or Aunt Betty's cancer.

Yet, here we encounter a strange and poignant paradox in the life of faith. Our prayers do not seem to be answered simply because we really want them to be answered. A popular writer on prayer has suggested half facetiously that we would be in a very sorry state if God gave us everything that we think we need or want. God's reasons and God's ways are not ours. There is no automatic relationship between the depth of our concern and the response (or the seeming lack of one) from God.

The laments of the psalms, both the individual and communal laments, move from distress to pleading, to an outburst of confidence in God's wondrous works and faithfulness. That is how the universe is supposed to be, isn't it? The individual or nation confesses its sin so that, in the renewed relationship with God, confidence in God's ultimate deliverance is restored. Perhaps, in ancient Israel, a cultic priest announced the promise of salvation to the assembly. But in these passages from Jeremiah, confession and intercession are followed not by a promise of deliverance, but by statements of judgment. God's answer to these prayers is a decisive no. "The LORD said to me, 'Even if Moses and Samuel stood before me, I would not be moved to pity this people' " (15:1a NEB). The apostasy of the nation has been too great and the events of the times too well set in motion for the clock of history to be turned back.

A friend of mine works at a hospice. Often we meet for morning coffee and check in with each other. Hers is the heavier expression, for the beginning of the day is already too much with her. Most of the residents in the hospice are young: AIDS victims, mothers with inoperable tumors, people with terminal disease. "Why is this happening to me?" they ask. "I want to live. Why is God letting this happen?" There seem to be no answers to such questions. Their rage and sorrow at their dying can only be met with silence and a compassion that holds a human being close when no words are adequate. Is God's answer to Jeremiah adequate? What is your response to God's answer to Jeremiah?

Jeremiah's confession (15:11ff.) is born out of the depths of his experience and emotions with the people and with God. You will note how some of these verses are similar in style to the laments we discussed above, but here Jeremiah is struggling with his own vocation as a prophet. It is likely that this confession comes late in his career.

What is this contention between God and Jeremiah? Elizabeth Achtemeier has written a paragraph, which I will quote in full because it seems so germane to our own life stories.

> Jeremiah is one here with every person who has lived in intimate fellowship with God and who, in the midst of danger or dispute, has taken a stand on the Word of God. He is one with Moses, defying an empire on the basis of that Word; one with Elijah, challenging a queen; one with Daniel, facing the lions; one with Luther, defying pope and electors; just as he is also one with a Bonhoeffer, saying no to a Hitler, and a Martin Luther King, Jr., challenging a nation. But he is also one with every ordinary Christian, who has ever

dared to defy society's convention and powers in the belief that the Word of God is true and that God's way and God's will shall finally triumph. Faithful souls stake their lives, their fortunes, their sacred honor on the belief that God will be true to his Word. But what if God proves not true? What if the Word is a lie and God will not fulfill it after all? What if the fountain of living waters is instead a temporary freshet that will dry up in the heat of the day? Is that not finally the question our Lord asked when he cried out from the cross, "My God, my God, why have you forsaken me?" "Wilt thou be to me like a deceitful brook, like waters that fail?" (*Jeremiah* 61)

Discussion and Action

1. Compare your styles of prayer with each other. How do they differ?
2. Is intercessory prayer a regular part of your prayer life? Why or why not? For whom? Who do you know who intercedes on your behalf?
3. When does your worshiping community use intercessory prayer? Would you like to see intercessory prayer incorporated into your corporate worship experience? How?
4. What qualifies someone to intercede with God on behalf of others? Who among you does not need intercessory prayer? Is it okay to pray for someone who doesn't want intercession? Why or why not?
5. Design an intercessory prayer service for the regular worship in your congregation. Offer it to the pastor to be used during worship.

6

Cost of Repentance
Jeremiah 18–20

The image of the potter is used to represent the way in which God views the people of God.

Personal Preparation

1. Read Jeremiah 18–20. In what way does the image of the potter make you feel as if you have failed? In what ways does it feel as if God is doing a new thing in you?
2. What can you defend about the way things are in the culture today? What would you personally condemn? Is there more to defend or condemn? Is there more for God to defend or condemn?
3. With God, good things can come out of bad situations. What good comes out of the disasters you have seen in life (personal disasters, natural disasters, community and national disasters)?
4. Is there anything you should not say to God in prayer? What would it be?

Understanding

Old Testament scholar Walter Brueggemann presents a provocative thesis in his 1984 Jordan Lectures. Running throughout the Bible are two major types of faith that exist together in considerable tension. On the one hand, there is the royal priestly tradition of continuity, the tradition of blessing and thankfulness for all the good that God has given. On the other hand, there is the prophetic tradition of accountability, the tradition of discontinuity. The central task of prophetic faith, Brueggemann argues, is to call us to examine the discontinuities, the things that no longer work in our lives, though we would very much like to live as if they did not matter or were working perfectly well, thank you.

Thus, Jeremiah is the prophet of the exile. In a sense, he calls people *to* the exile. If 587 B.C. is the date of the fall of Judah, the destruction of the Jerusalem temple, and the political disintegration of the Israelites, it is the pivotal date in Old Testament history. It is the task of the prophet to get the people to experience that date and history not only as God's judgment of the people, but also as the beginning of a new history, a new faithfulness. To do this the people will have to let go of the world as they know it, as they have organized it. That world has been destroyed. It is now the movement of faith to relinquish the world that has been, in order to participate in the new world to which God calls the faithful. Brueggemann already finds the key words for this work of the prophet in the first chapter of Jeremiah in which God calls Jeremiah to his vocation:

> See, today I appoint you over nations and over kingdoms,
> to *pluck up* and to *pull down*,
> to *destroy* and to *overthrow*,
> to *build* and to *plant*. (1:10)

Four heavy verbs and two hopeful verbs are at the heart of Jeremiah's ministry, Brueggemann argues, and in that order.

I began with Brueggemann's contentions because almost immediately in the symbol of the potter of chapter 18 we encounter the push of Jeremiah's calling.

> Then the word of the LORD came to me: "Can I not do with you, O house of Israel, just as this potter has done?" says the LORD. "Just like the clay in the potter's hand, so are you in my hand, O house of Israel. At one moment I may declare concerning a nation or a kingdom, that I will *pluck up* and *break down* and *destroy* it, but if that nation . . . turns from its evil, I will change

my mind about the disaster I intended to bring on it."(18:5-8)

Jeremiah is sent by God to watch a potter make some pots. The potter works and works, and if it doesn't come out right then the potter smashes the clay and starts over. God can do what God thinks is necessary to get a thing right. God can have a change of mind about Israel that would be far from the expected or pleasant. Or, as Walter Brueggemann puts it, "See, this is how it is between me and my people and I'm going to keep working it until I get it right and if it doesn't turn out right I'm going to smash it." Verse 12 of chapter 18 seems to be Jeremiah's view that the people will be too stubborn to listen to God, but at this point it appears, at least, that Judah still does have a choice in the matter.

By skipping ahead to chapter 19, we can see that a very similar mood dominates verses 1-13. Indeed, chapters 18–20 involve a parallelism around the smashing of pottery: warnings, warnings unheeded, disaster foretold, God's messenger in danger, and the two concluding confessions.

Parallel structure:

18:1-10 pottery making	19:1-13 pottery smashing
18:11-17 shaping disaster	19:14-15 bringing disaster
18:18 let's attack him	20:1-6 let's lock him up
18:19-23 Lord, they are after me	20:7-18 Lord, it's them . . . and you, too.

The confession of Jeremiah 20:7-18 is the fifth and last of Jeremiah's confessional utterances. It needs to be read aloud to catch the full weight of Jeremiah's pain. How audacious of Jeremiah to begin with such strong words to God! Scholars are not convinced that these words were composed following the beatings and imprisonment described in Jeremiah 20:1-6, but that story certainly adds to the urgency of the prophet's cry to God. What does Jeremiah mean by his cry that God has deceived him (some commentators would have us read "seduced")? Is there any language that is unacceptable when addressed to God? Or, is authentic prayer life open to the fullest expression of our needs and feelings?

Unfortunately, Jeremiah's contemporaries had neither the wisdom of hindsight nor the faithfulness to change, and so the catastrophe of 587 B.C. came with unrelieved horror. God had to smash the clay in order to make of it a worthy vessel. Judah was unwilling to see that its world of covenantal faithfulness had in fact already disappeared. God had withdrawn the blessing that held that world together. Now, only from the radically ruptured community in exile would the new word from God begin to take shape.

Jeremiah's pain, shouted out to God, is the pain of one who knows of impending catastrophe and is increasingly helpless to change it. Yet, the pain of the first verse turns, like a lament psalm, to a singing of God's praise and so ends with the triumphal verse 13. We witness Jeremiah's personal pain and then a claim of God's faithfulness to all the poor, that is, to all those who have no stake in maintaining the present order against the signs of collapse and faithlessness.

Verses 14-20 must have originally been part of a separate confession for they do not follow from the confidence of verse 13. They seem to reverse the mood completely. Some have remarked that only in Job do we find anything approaching the desolation of these verses. Perhaps, as Lawrence Boadt notes, it was meant to be the final comment of despair over the necessity of exile "in which Jeremiah's personal suffering becomes representative of the nation as a whole" (*Jeremiah 1–25* 154). Taken together, the two parts of this confession reveal the violent swings of mood in the journey of faith, from buoyant confidence to utter aloneness, a journey that we all experience.

Have we not known with a certain clarity those moments when the design of this world (if only our personal world) is exactly as it should be? The pottery is beautiful. We are blessed indeed! But then something changes. Perhaps an illness or a loss in death or the death of a relationship means that old loved world is gone. A new way of being must emerge if we are to be faithful. And how painful that new way of being is in its emergence. Still, the struggle toward newness is not done in isolation. God is the potter who reworks what is now broken. That vessel shall be worthy.

Discussion and Action

1. Recall Brueggemann's descriptions of the "royal priestly" and "prophetic" traditions. What, generally, is the tone or mood of your faith community's worship? Is it more of the royal priestly type or more of the prophetic type?
2. What can you defend about the way things are in the culture today? What would you personally condemn? Is there more to defend or condemn? Is there more for God to defend or condemn?
3. Discuss the following statement: "In wealthy countries God is generally perceived as the bestower of blessings, but in poorer countries God is known as the one who liberates."
4. When has God reworked your life so that you emerged a new and more faithful person?
5. Work with clay of any kind. Try to make perfect spheres, cubes, or other three-dimensional shapes. How difficult is it to make something perfect? What would a perfect humanity look like?

True or False Prophets
Jeremiah 23:9-40; 27–28

How do we recognize the true prophets in our time? How do we distinguish between true and false prophecy?

Personal Preparation

1. Read Jeremiah 23:9-40; 27–28. Who are your favorite Christian writers and speakers? Why do you prefer them to others? Which of them agree with what you think? Which ones challenge your thinking?
2. What false prophets do you know of in our society? How do you know what they're saying is untrue?
3. How do you account for the fact that others interpret scripture differently from you? Who's right? Who's wrong?
4. If you were going to preach a sermon, what would you say? To what extent would you give people an encouraging word? To what extent would you tell them the painful truth?

Understanding

In her article "How to Read the Bible Prayerfully," Sandra M. Schneiders, I.H.M., argues that the Christian movement known as fundamentalism rests on three erroneous presuppositions. The first error is the belief that inspiration means that the exact wording of a book was given to Jeremiah, say, as we have it now.

Secondly, fundamentalism claims to be able to read the text at face value, to read it exactly for what the words mean.

To me, however, Schneiders' most important argument is the third: "The fundamentalist takes a magical view of the text. Magic is an attempt to make God conform to our will by the performance of certain behaviors. God has given us no assurance that if we read the Bible with unnuanced naivete God will infallibly supply us with divine truth" *(The Bible Today,* Vol. 22, No. 2, p. 2). In many ways, "magic" is not only an attempt to secure God's favor, it is also an attempt to make the world safer. A world filled with anxieties, doubts, and rapid change calls forth in all of us a deep need for stability, connectedness, and absolutes. It may seem to us that the terror of personal and political disintegration can be arrested only if we can discover (rediscover) those values and beliefs which seem to be cloaked in "the absolute security of a divine Word grasped fundamentalistically" (Eugene LaVerdieve, *The Bible Today.* Vol. 21, No. 1, p. 3).

The relevance of this argument for the Book of Jeremiah goes beyond a plea for a nonliteralist reading of the text. It is apparent that Judah during the life of Jeremiah was a country besieged by troubles from within and without. On Judah's borders were the imperialist advances of the Babylonian empire. With Babylon's victory the political, social, and religious conventions of Judah's life would be over. The known world was coming to an end. In the extremity of the situation can there be any wonder that the temptation to "magic" would be very strong? What was required to placate God, to secure peace, and to put the people's hearts at rest?

Something more important than moralistic preaching is going on in Jeremiah. The issue of false prophets has to do with authenticity of the word which, after all, can speak for God and to the issue, as I mentioned, of how one faces into the insecurities and anxieties of the times. How, indeed, is this to be done in a way that is not an attempt to secure God's favorable actions and blessings? Given the pressures of the times, how is one able to proclaim God's word rather than projecting one's own needs and hopes onto God? These are apparently the crucial questions when we examine the central section of 23:9-40.

> These are the words of the LORD of Hosts:
> "Do not listen to what the prophets say, who buoy you
>   up with false hopes;
> the vision they report springs from their own imagi-
>   nation,
> it is not from the mouth of the LORD.
>
> "They say to those who spurn the word of the LORD,
> 'Prosperity shall be yours';
> and to all who follow the promptings of their own stub-
>   born heart they say,
> 'No disaster shall befall you.'
> But which of them has stood in the council of the
>   LORD . . . ?" (Jer. 23:16-18a NEB)

Clearly, Jeremiah wants to differentiate his ministry from the ministry of other prophets, who also claim to speak on God's behalf. And so Jeremiah lists three characteristics of what he considers false prophecy. First, false prophets do not speak God's word. Their word is not based on revelation or spiritual intimacy. It is a word which they have made up. Secondly, their false words are based upon a fundamental flaw within themselves. Finally, false prophecy is based upon giving the people what they want to hear, a message of hope and encouragement. It is a message of complacency, of prosperity; it does not challenge those who "spurn the way of the Lord."

Elizabeth Achtemeier calls the false prophets of Jeremiah's time—who, instead of criticizing the structure of things, seek and deliver God's blessing on it—"the preachers of success religion. . . . They are agents of the status quo . . . they cannot mediate new life to their hearers, because they find nothing wrong with the old . . . they simply fill them with the vain hope that they are already right with God" (*Jeremiah* 77).

One period of American history when this nation seemed to be right with God was in the years closely following World War II.

An enemy had been defeated. The United States was at its height in economic, political, and military power. For the most part, the situation at home was good: there were jobs, churches were filled, and new churches were being built. But the peace of the times was shattered when the Soviet Union exploded their first atomic device. A new enemy was emerging, the specter of an international godless communist threat. A new postwar military buildup was needed and soon the nuclear arms race was on its way. Even in my small hometown in the northern part of the state of Washington, local citizens scanned the skies to see if any Soviet bombers were flying overhead. In the meantime, to be ready a national alert was ordered. A nuclear war between the good and evil empires was possible. However, survival was also possible if precautions were taken. In New York a statewide civil defense drill was ordered in 1955; it was illegal not to participate. Violators would be sentenced up to a year in jail and fined five hundred dollars.

Who would refuse to participate? Civil defense seemed like sound practical advice. Yet, there were many who refused to participate in these "safety drills." One of these was Dorothy Day, a founder of the Catholic Worker Movement. Her biographer, Jim Forest, explains, "Dorothy emphasized that her refusal to take shelter was not only a protest against war and preparations for war, but an 'act of penance' undertaken by an American whose country 'had been the first to drop the atom bomb and make the hydrogen bomb.' " She was arrested several times for her crime. Now civil defense from nuclear war seems a bit ludicrous, but in the 1950s it was taken very seriously. The protestors were ridiculed at first and thought by some to be just a little crazy. God's position on the subject was so obvious to the sane observer.

The false prophets viewed truth as a possession. They believed that truth could be found in the culture and the religion in which they were immersed and that God (truth) can, in fact, be identified with the prevailing opinions and behavior.

To such views God clearly answers: "Am I a God nearby . . . and not a God far off?" (23:23). Lawrence Boadt comments, "God is *not* a deity near at hand; [God] is indeed far off. This may strike us strangely, for the search to find God nearby characterizes the modern religious mentality. Jeremiah, however, wants to remind his audience that God cannot be grabbed hold of, cannot be treated in human terms . . . Yahweh is no local divinity, but master of creation" (*Jeremiah 1–25* 190).

Discussion and Action

1. Identify any instances of false prophecy today.
2. By what standards are believers able to determine what is true and what is false prophecy?
3. Are there places in your immediate situation, either in your personal life, in your church, or in your community, that need to hear a prophetic word? What would that word be?
4. Who do you think would listen to the prophetic word?
5. Name situations where the church or the nation has used God to justify behavior that was really self-serving?
6. Is God democratic? If a majority of the people believe the same thing about God, is that proof it's true? Why or why not?

8

Witnessing to God's Word
Jeremiah 36

Jeremiah's stand against the political and religious leaders of his time offers us a model for our own relationship to the status quo.

Personal Preparation

1. Read Jeremiah 36. Think of a setback in your life. What were your options? Why did you persevere?
2. What do you think God is feeling about the church? governments? other religions? wars? What are your feelings? Where are they the same as God's? Where are they different?
3. Would you say you usually "stick to your guns" in arguments, or do you finally say "If you can't beat 'em, join 'em"? How do you feel at the end of the argument?
4. When have you been unable to make church authorities, civic authorities, or government authorities listen to a prophetic message? What did you do?

Understanding

Josiah, the reforming king of whom Jeremiah had a generally favorable view, was followed in kingship by three of his sons. Of these, Jeremiah had very little good to say. In particular, Jeremiah heaped scorn on Jehoiakim, a king who ruled in acquiescence to Egypt (while his half-brother Jehoahaz, who had previously been king, was being held in Egypt). It was not simply the political

alignment that Jeremiah found offensive, but the very style of
Jehoiakim's rule.

According to the oracle of Jeremiah 22:13-19, Jehoiakim ruled
with an insensitivity to the condition of his people who were already suffering under the heavy tributes that Judah was paying to
Egypt. While his country was reeling under the scarcity of resources, Jehoiakim attempted to emulate the pomp and glory of
his predecessors who ruled when Israel was both independent
and economically secure. Further, true kingship, in Jeremiah's
view, was grounded in the covenantal nature of Israel's relationship with God. It would not express itself so much in monarchi-
cal finery or governmental pomp, but through "knowing God,"
especially the knowledge of God that shows itself through justice.

Jeremiah's words in this oracle end with a note of utter contempt. Because of Jehoiakim's concern for splendor rather than
the well-being of his people, he will become as nothing in the
memory of Israel: "They shall not lament for him, saying, 'Alas,
lord!' or 'Alas, his majesty!' With the burial of a donkey he shall
be buried—dragged off and thrown out beyond the gates of
Jerusalem" (22:18b-19). Is that any way to talk about the ruler
of a nation?

Dr. Charles Clements, a Quaker and physician, spent nearly a
year in the liberated zones of El Salvador providing medical aid
to the victims of that nation's civil war and poverty. When he
returned to the U.S., he wrote and spoke about his experiences
and his opposition to the policies of the U.S. in Central America.
At one such appearance, which I attended, a local pastor gave the
introductory prayer. A sentence of that prayer caused some com-
motion during this supposedly quiet time: "God forgive this country for electing fools to high ranking offices." That line created
both some chuckling and some discomfort. It hardly seemed like
a respectful thing to say about the president of our country, let
alone to say it in a prayer! But really, how different is that prayer
from the verbal abuse Jeremiah heaped on Jehoiakim? A burial
fit for a jackass . . .

To understand the audacity of prophetic utterance to the powers that be, we need to keep in mind the essential aspects of the

prophetic vocation. To repeat an earlier observation, biblical prophecy is not about predicting the future, and the work of the prophet is not that of foretelling the coming Messiah. Certainly, New Testament authors gleaned material from the prophets to explain who Jesus was (Jesus himself was well aware of the prophets), but that says little about the intention of the prophets. The prophets were figures who emerged in times of acute historical crisis in the life of Israel—primarily the destruction of the Northern Kingdom by the Assyrians in 722 B.C. (Amos and Hosea) and the destruction of Jerusalem by the Babylonians in 587 B.C. (Jeremiah and Ezekiel).

The message of the prophets was directed to the elite (the religious, political, and economic leaders) whose lack of fidelity to the covenant and failure to act with justice were putting Israel on a collision course with historical destruction. The foolish (and dangerous) pretenses of the elite had to be exposed. The poor were suffering. The official prophets were telling lies. The leaders of the nation had exchanged covenantal relationship with God for (supposed) cultural and political stability. This coming destruction was in fact a judgment by God, and unless Israel repented and returned to their God, the destruction would occur.

In *Jesus, A New Vision*, Marcus Borg says, "[The Prophets'] passion about their people's life in history had as its primary source their communion with God. Their relationship to the Spirit led them to see things from a perspective very different from the dominant consciousness. Moreover, they did not simply *see* differently; they also *felt* differently. They not only knew God, but *felt* the *feelings* of God: the divine compassion for the victims of suffering, the anger of God at the oppressing classes, the divine grief about the suffering that would soon come upon victimizer and victim alike." Being messengers of God meant that the prophets would have to address the ruling parties; they would be obligated to do so in spite of the isolation and opposition that such speaking would cause. Perhaps the fact that so few listened was even more painful to the prophets than direct persecution. There is a story about a young person who asked an elder why it was that he continued year after year to preach and give warnings when it was so obvious that no one was listening. The elder replied that he didn't preach so much to change others, but so that he wouldn't be changed. Faithfulness makes demands upon the prophetic voice.

The story of chapter 36 is a wonderful illustration of the powerful leader's (Jehoiakim's) contempt for the preaching of the prophets. With complete confidence and disdain, Jehoiakim burns the oracles of God that Jeremiah has dictated to his scribe Baruch. No doubt the powerful king found the power of the prophetic word to be an easily neglected thing. It is a gesture of imperious heights. Jeremiah's powerful word is simply laughable to the king.

What is the recourse for the faithful when the powerful refuse to listen? What will gain the attention of the ruling elite? Letters? Phone calls? Marches? Prayers? Acts of civil disobedience? And how is it that the faithful can invoke the power of God in a way that both exposes the emperor and honors God? How to act and speak with urgency but without desperation? In what ways can the prophetic voice reveal the anger, the pain, and the compassion of God? And, do different historical situations call for different ways of speaking? Who will speak, what words will be said, what actions will be taken when there is no food for children while the rich are pampering their pets? What militaries have destroyed the only clinic for hundreds of miles, when you are forced to live in segregation because of the color of your skin, when public funds that could be used for healing wounds are only spent in making new and ingenious weapons that cause wounds? How then shall the voice of God be heard?

Discussion and Action

1. When and to whom do the leaders of our government listen?
2. How important a role would you give protest in the life of faith?
3. What does it mean that Christians sometimes speak on the opposite sides of public issues?
4. Are there some ways of protesting that you feel dishonor God and so are counter to the vision of faith? What are they?

9

Instilling Hope
Jeremiah 37; 32

*At the very moment the future looked the darkest,
Jeremiah bought a plot of land in his home town of
Anathoth. How do we experience hope in the midst
of despair?*

Personal Preparation

1. Read Jeremiah 37 and 32. How much confidence do you
   have in the future? How much better or worse will things
   be for the next generation and the generation after that?
2. What are you doing in your life to plan for the future
   despite the possibility that there could be economic collapse, war, a natural disaster, disease, or a fatal accident
   in your future?
3. How near have you come to despair in your life? Where
   did you look for hope?
4. Why do you think God allows horrible things to happen
   to people?

Understanding

Ironweed, a movie based on a novel of the same name by William
Kennedy, is difficult to watch. It's the story of Francis Phelan, a
former baseball player but now alcoholic and a self-proclaimed
bum, who returns to his hometown, Albany, New York, after an
absence of more than twenty years. While there he is confronted

by a number of ghosts reminding him of past painful experiences. But the memory of his dead infant son haunts him the most. Twenty years earlier Francis accidentally dropped his infant son and the baby died. It was likely that Francis had been drinking.Unable to face his guilt and loss, Phelan left his family and had not returned until now. In the movie's most powerful scene, Phelan shows up at his former home with a twelve-and-a-half-pound turkey. With surprising ease and grace, his ex-wife invites him in for supper. His daughter, however, is not able to conceal her anger at her father's sudden return. She says, "Do you think you can just show up here after all these years? Do you think you can just walk in here and be forgiven? Forgiveness isn't that easy."

Phelan responds, "I'm way past forgiving."

The movie ends with an ambiguous scene. Is Phelan throwing the bottle away because he realizes finally that his ghosts are not hidden by his drunkenness, that they will continue to find him no matter where or how he hides? Perhaps, but the total mood of the film gives little credence to even that small sense of hope. The real sense one has from this movie is that it is about a man who has run out of reasons to live. Earlier in the film another "bum" says to Phelan, "I'm still alive."

Phelan answers, "That's what you think." It's an answer he could have given to himself. He feels himself past forgiveness.

Jean Paul Sartre entitled his play about hell *No Exit*. It's a good metaphor for hell. Life without hope is a life that seems to have no place to go. We know that Jeremiah lived on both sides of the traumatic destruction of the temple and the exile into Babylon. Jeremiah pleaded on behalf of God for Judah to change, to return to God in order that the painful experiences of 587 B.C. could be avoided. At exactly the point when there seemed to be no hope, when destruction and exile seemed an only too clear sign that God had given up on Israel, that Israel was past forgiving, Jeremiah's voice is filled with hope. This week's readings look at the possibility of hope in a time of hopelessness.

Some historical background will help us understand what is going on in these chapters. A few years before the destruction of the temple, Judah was ruled by its last king, Zedekiah. When the

Babylonian (Chaldean) siege of Jerusalem is suddenly lifted because of increased military and political activity by Egypt, a great sense of hope is created, and it appears that Jeremiah's warnings were the babblings of a pessimist, if not a traitor. Surely, God has delivered Judah from the clutches of its enemies. People are finally free to roam beyond the city's walls. Jeremiah himself is on his way to his hometown, Anathoth, a few miles north of Jerusalem. At one of the city gates, Jeremiah is arrested by a member of the king's guards, flogged, and thrown into prison. The charge is treason, not a totally unrealistic charge given that Jeremiah had often counseled that a Babylonian victory was assured. Moreover, Jeremiah's latest oracle was that the sense of hope Judah felt in Babylon's lifting of the blockade was illusory. To the king, Jeremiah preached that the Babylonians would return, and with biting irony he adds, "Even if you defeated the whole army of Chaldeans (Babylonians) who are fighting against you, and there remained of them only wounded men in their tents, they would rise up and burn this city with fire" (37:10).

Reading chapter 37 first gives much greater power to Jeremiah's strange purchase in chapter 32. Now we are much closer to the fateful events of 587 B.C. Jerusalem is again completely under siege. Without doubt, conditions under the Babylonian blockade would have been horrifying. Food and water would have been rationed; disease would have been rampant, partly due to the resultant malnutrition. In the midst of this desperate situation, when the inevitability of Babylonian victory would have been obvious to even the most ardent nationalist, Jeremiah performs what must have amounted to a parabolic act: he purchases land for the future.

Walter Brueggemann describes Jeremiah as a poet of hope. Because our usual predilection is to ground our security in the way things are, to defend and maintain the status quo, we cannot imagine a newness that will emerge if our present world and way of life crumbles. In *The Hopeful Imagination*, Brueggemann comments: "Jeremiah's vitality comes precisely from his passionate conviction about the power of God to work a newness in the zero hour of loss and exile. Jeremiah does not believe the world is hopelessly closed so that living is only moving the pieces around. Jeremiah bears witness to the work of God, the capacity to bring a newness *ex nihilo* [i.e., "out of nothing"]. For that reason loss and emptiness are not the last word."

Perhaps the real challenge of Jeremiah's parabolic action is that it finally represents a complete abandonment to trust in God's faithfulness, a sense that, despite all indications to the contrary, God will provide. This is far from a sigh of resignation. Rather, it is a statement of confidence in God's dynamic presence.

Discussion and Action

1. Consider this statement: Hope has two lovely daughters— anger and courage. In what way is this a helpful or an unhelpful description of hope? Is there room for anger in hope?

2. Tell some of the ways you plan for the future despite the possibility you won't live to see it. How do you feel about working for a future that only others will enjoy?

3. Share experiences in your life in which you felt that you were at a dead end, but then something caused a sense of newness and hope. How did that happen? Who or what was the messenger of that hope?

4. Is hope a pervading sense of your life, or the life of your church? If so, why? If not, what seems to be blocking that hope?

5. Buy a little land. With purchased potting soil, start a few garden plants or flower seeds or force flower bulbs to sprout early. Offer bulbs to the worship committee of your congregation for use in a worship center.

Prad 22:3

10

Renewing Covenant
Jeremiah 31

A new covenant emerged out of the utter desolation of Israel's existence. We discover that exile can lead to return, just as the cross leads to resurrection and new life.

Personal Preparation

1. Read chapter 31 aloud to yourself. Go back and underline or copy the words and phrases that describe God. Which images are most meaningful to you personally?
2. What have been the greatest sorrows in your life and your greatest joys? How are these individual incidences related, if at all?
3. If real joy comes only from real sorrow, what should you think about sorrow? When, if ever, have you looked forward to sorrow? Good Friday and Easter? The comfort of death for someone in pain? What was that experience like?
4. In what ways are you in denial about the state of the environment, your age, your health, and poverty and wealth in the world?

Understanding

I have a friend who was sexually abused as a child. She continues to be gripped by feelings of terror and helplessness, reminders of the panic she experienced many years ago. Still, those moments are not as strong or as frequent as they used to be. Therapy and the passage of time have helped. Hope is being fulfilled as the pain of that terrible family experience is being transformed by the healing experiences of intimacy, joy, and self-acceptance.

We all know people who have experienced the pain that accompanies the ending of a relationship. Marriage was nearly inviolable in the church only a few years ago, but now suffers from the scarring of divorce in numbers not unlike that of the larger society. But it is the personal tragedy of divorce, rather than the general societal problem, that touches us most. The loneliness, hopelessness, anger, guilt, and pain can seem overwhelming to the two people involved and to those of us who walk with them. Still, the hope of a new life beyond loss gradually emerges as genuinely new life. New relationships and strengths are discovered. Self-esteem grows.

People involved in substance abuse often feel trapped by their behavior. Yet, the beginning of a cure is that moment when they know they are trapped and they begin to hope for a drug-free world—the moment of the first stirrings that they do not have to live the old way forever.

Somehow, the structure of hope is similar in all cases. It is a hope for a new reality that powers the coming of that new reality itself. It is, in this sense, a **real**istic hope, a hope that becomes **actual**ized. Thus, hope is far different from a fantasy or a daydream. Genuine hope seems to have this power to push us or move us in the direction of that for which we hope. Hope may not even be enjoyable, for hope may demand of us, may pull out of us, changes of behavior and beliefs that can cause conflict with our old selves or the old world from which we are moving. Hope is something more than a pipe dream. Hope is not the last gasp when all else has failed. Hope is the beginning of something new. To use an old phrase, desire and fulfillment are intimately related.

Jeremiah 31 has to do with grieving and rejoicing, with being lost and being found, with leaving and returning. "These are the words of the Lord: 'Cease your loud weeping, shed no more tears;

for there shall be a reward for your toil, they shall return from the land of the enemy' " (31:1b NEB). The days of exile and bondage will end and hope will be realized through the faithfulness of God. Walter Brueggemann forcefully reminds us, however, that such hope does not come easily. As pastors and writers often remark during Holy Week, there is no resurrection without the cross. Brueggemann would have us add that there is no return without the exile, no hope without grief. Genuine and authentic hope, unlike a more shallow optimism, does not avoid the painful realities of existence but wrestles and struggles with those realities in the light of hope's promises.

Joanna Macy and others have shown that, in facing the threat of nuclear weapons, the greatest obstacle to hope-filled action as opposed to silent resignation is not simply the magnitude and the complexity of the nuclear arms race. Rather, the horror of a possible nuclear extinction has so impinged upon our minds as to overwhelm us. The result of this emotional burden is what Robert Jay Lifton has termed "psychic numbing," a pain so scary, a threat so real that the first act of protection is to "bury" this terrible information deep inside of us so that we will not have to deal with it, a kind of radical denial system. It is necessary first to work through this emotional trauma of facing the existence of nuclear weapons before we will be able to work socially and politically in opposition to nuclear arms. This grief work, this cry of pain, is the first act that frees us for a hope-filled commitment to a nuclear-free world.

We might say that the destruction of the temple and the exile into Babylon were the nuclear holocaust of Judah in the sixth century B.C. The expulsion of God's people from the promised land is the psychic-numbing, perhaps we should say, the faith-numbing experience of the Israelites. It is the work of the prophet, Brueggemann argues, to bring that painful experience to the consciousness of his fellow citizens. The word of the prophet allows the grief work to begin in order that real hope might emerge. In *The Prophetic Imagination,* Brueggemann comments on Jeremiah 31:15:

> *A voice is heard in Ramah, lamentation and bitter*
> *weeping. Rachel is weeping for her children; she re-*
> *fuses to be comforted by her children, because they*
> *are not* (RSV).

Neither Jeremiah nor his contemporaries are adequate
to this grief. It must be done by the one who in anguish gave birth and in anguish now faces death. There
is no comfort anymore; not comforted: they are not!
The death of the unthinkable end is matched to the
birth of the unthinkable miracle of beginning. Now it
has been said. They are not; not exiled; not punished.
Just *not*! And that is beyond consolation or explanation. This poetry is among the boldest in ancient Israel, for the situation requires audacity. Imagine bringing back mother Rachel to grieve her darling. There
can only be grief . . . Yahweh himself is grieving and
will not turn loose. (57-58)

Our recognition of God's grief allows us to face into our own.
Although the possibility of a grieving God has sometimes been
labeled the heresy of Patri-passionism (literally, "the father who
suffers"), we would have to say that in the Bible there are abundant images of a God who feels, and feels passionately. Such passion for Christians is revealed finally on the cross. There the image of grief on Good Friday is transformed and becomes the joy
of new life at Easter. But there can be no resurrection without the
cross, there can be no return without exile.

Still, return there is! God does not abandon the people forever.
A new covenant emerges out of what can be described only as
utter desolation. God takes a broken "no people" and transforms
them into a new people with a new covenant. The sinful past will
be forgotten. There will be a new and deeper relationship between
God and the faithful. It will be a relationship which exists at the
very core of a person, at the place of the heart. This is nothing the
people were able to do for themselves, as the sad story of the
rejection of the prophetic word has made clear. Rather, God has

done this, and it is a work born of much love, many tears, and great faithfulness.

Discussion and Action

1. Do you believe that God is capable of tears? Why, or why not?
2. Is God transforming you or your faith community? What issues/things/people are you avoiding, those that must be dealt with before you can truly be open to God's presence?
3. Why can't people change before situations turn disastrous?
4. Julian of Norwich, in a famous image, has described Jesus as our mother. It is an image that is to show us "indwelling in Christ" through stages of birthing, nurturing, protecting. Finally, such an image shows God's mothering care for a stumbling child. What is your image of God when you stumble? Is it that of a mother who waits to hold you in her arms? Or, will there be much scolding? or both?
5. Brainstorm ways that you could practice exile so that you can also experience a joyous return. "Exile" yourself from friends for a week, then have a meal together to celebrate. Or deny yourself something you enjoy—reading, television, movies, sweets.

Suggestions for Sharing and Prayer

This material is designed for covenant groups that spend one hour sharing and praying together, followed by one hour of Bible study. This section was written by the Reverend Cathy Myers Wirt, consultant for Small Group Ministries, Christian Church (Disciples of Christ).

Prayer and sharing time offers the Bible study group an opportunity to move learning from our heads to our hearts. Our biblical text, the Book of Jeremiah, makes that invitation as well, inviting the hearer to move the law from head to heart, to literally have the word written on our hearts (Jer. 31:33). To this end, I propose a rhythm for our sharing and prayer that is heart-centered. The seven movements for the sharing time include: Opening our hearts, Listening with our hearts, Taking heart, Enlarging our hearts, Heart to heart with God, With a song in our hearts, and Words from God's heart.

Opening our hearts means preparing to receive the gifts of learning and scripture. To begin your time together each week, I suggest singing the chant on page 71 of this book, "Write these words in our hearts." You may also choose another song/chant or prayer that is meaningful to your group.

Listening with our hearts means looking into the text, seeking what is most needed for each person in your group to grow in their faith. Begin by creating a giant heart from paper, fabric, cardboard, clay, or whatever material you choose. At the beginning of each sharing and prayer time, invite everyone in the group to write on or attach a message to the heart. Use words from the week's scripture lesson that each participant believes he/she most needs to have written on his/her heart at this point in life.

Once the words are attached, ask each person, if they wish, to share why that word affects them this week in their particular circumstance. What might God be yearning to teach through these words of scripture?

Taking heart means giving encouragement to our sisters and brothers of faith or people to whom we are reaching out in love. Find a specific way to affirm others and practice it each week as a group. For example, you may choose to send a heart imprinted with a message from the group to people in your congregation or to visitors to your congregation. These hearts could be made with stampers, affixing stickers on cards, clay, cookies, origami paper-folding, woven paper, batik, chocolate molds, computer pictures, cupcakes, sponge painting on cloth or Bible covers. Also, making cinnamon hearts is easy and inexpensive. Let your group find its own way of encouraging others to take heart.

Cinnamon Hearts

In a bowl, mix $1/3$ c. nontoxic white glue, $1\ 1/2$ cups cinnamon and 1 cup of applesauce until it forms a ball. You will have to work the mixture for quite a while. Chill the mixture for at least 30 minutes or overnight, though much more than 8 hours makes the dough tough to work with. Use a rolling pin to roll out the dough $1/4$" thick. Cut out hearts with a heart-shaped cookie cutter and sprinkle each heart with cinnamon. Put them in a warm place to dry, preferably on a wire rack, for two days. If you want to use the cookie as an ornament, you can put a small hole in the heart before it is dry; then thread a ribbon through the hole to hang the heart. These cinnamon hearts will add fragrance to any room for almost three years.

Enlarging our hearts means looking at the scripture through a new method. For each chapter I will be suggesting several ways to approach the text experientially.

Heart to heart with God is what I have named the group prayer time. You might choose to have a method of prayer that remains the same for all ten weeks, or you might choose to vary the prayer time. I have suggested one prayer method for each session, but you will find the natural prayer way for your group.

With a song in our hearts we rejoice before and with God's presence. Some Covenant groups have found their own song that enhances their unity as a group. If you do not have a musician in your group, you could ask a musician from your congregation to record an accompaniment to your song/songs. Several hymns are provided here.

Words from God's heart may be used as a benediction at closing. By having your last words be the same each time, you create a space for these words to be written on your heart in a special way. Choose your closing or benediction and print them on large sheets of paper and put them in the middle of your circle so that you can all see them as you join together at closing. I suggest Jeremiah 31:33; Jeremiah 29:11-14; or Jeremiah 17:14.

1. Called to Miinistry

Enlarging our hearts

❑ Jeremiah 1:1-3 describes the author and his context by naming his parents, vocation, location, place in history, government leaders of his day, the amount of time covered in the text, and a major historical event to which to tie the scripture. Using these verses as a model, ask each participant to write his or her own context, listing full name, the names of parents, vocation, place of birth, and current residence, the season of the year in which you are beginning this study, a listing of several influential leaders of the day, and a major historical event that has occurred and shapes the way we see the world. Share your contexts, comparing them with Jeremiah's and with each other. What similarities and dissimilarities do you note?

❑ The text talks of being known even before birth. Read the words to the contemporary hymn "I was there to hear your borning cry" (p. 70). What line of the hymn strikes you? Why do you think you are moved by that line?

❑ When Jeremiah explains to God the barriers to his sharing of the prophecy he was given, God moves the barriers aside.

Cover a box with paper of a solid color, and decorate the box with all of the excuses you use to not share the word of God. Make a wall out of all these boxes, and then dismantle the wall. You might want to keep this wall of boxes for your prayer focus for the full ten weeks.

❑ With soft music playing or in a quiet space, recall in your mind's eye a time when you were able to offer just the right word of hope to someone in a time of hopelessness. What does it feel like to see yourself as a messenger for God's love and grace?

❑ Jeremiah speaks in metaphors. List all of the metaphors in Jeremiah 1:1-19. Now practice seeing in metaphors. Place ten items of your choice on a table in front of the group. Pick up an item and see if you can see a message of God's presence in it. For example, I might pick up a rock and speak about the firm foundation of faith in my life. I might pick up a candle and talk about God's burning presence that brings light. Some people do not think in metaphors, but it is important to note that metaphors are Jeremiah's language.

Heart to heart with God

❑ Practice a breath prayer together. Concentrate on slowing and deepening your breathing. As you breathe in, say in your heart: "Before I formed you." As you breath out, say in your heart: "I knew you." You may choose to have instrumental music playing while you do this.

2. Living Water or Cracked Cisterns

Enlarging our hearts

❑ In Jeremiah 2 the author speaks of putting trust in the wrong places and not trusting in the everlasting God. The image used is of a cistern that won't hold water. Take ten paper cups and put holes of various sizes in the bottoms of them. Each person takes a cup and stands in a line. The last person in line should have a bowl instead of a cup, and the first person in line should have a pitcher of water. On the word *go*, the person with the pitcher pours water into the cup of the next person in line; then that person transfers as much water as possible to the next person, and so on, so that the water has touched all the cups. See how much water can be transported through the line of holey (and holy) cups. Unpack this metaphor. What does it mean when we are not secure vessels for carrying water? What happens when we trust in people or lifestyles that "don't hold water"?

❑ Make small clay pots with cracks in them to place in your homes reminding you of the folly of carrying faith in a broken vessel. Talk about the places in your life where hope drains out. How might you repair that part of your life, heart, or mind to make your faith stronger? How can the group help?

❑ Jeremiah 5:21 reminds us that we often do not see and do not hear what is right in front of us. Using a jigsaw puzzle that is not too large, divide the pieces and work the puzzle in silence together. Debrief this experience as a metaphor. What was it like to watch the picture emerge? How did you need each other? How frustrated did you get, or how joyful was the process? When we put together our visions of God in our midst, is the process at all similar? Can we help each other see and hear God? How?

❑ Jeremiah 5:23-24 talks about stubbornness in the face of a God who is visible in nature. Share stories of times you have been stubborn. What has it cost you in relationships or other rewards?

❑ Jeremiah 6:13-14 deals with false hopes given by leaders of the times. List some false hopes uttered in the news the past week. How do you weigh hopeful sounding words and determine what is false hope and what is genuine hope? False hope is frequently offered to people so they will not focus on a problem, but it does not offer a solution. (It is crying peace when there is no peace.)

Try writing statements of false hope and statements of genuine hope. For example: A false hope statement would be "I think it will turn out all right in the end." A genuine hope statement would be "I believe God's love is present in this circumstance, though I am not always sure where God is leading me." False hope is an everything-is-fine tone in the presence of events that *are not* fine. It has a hollow ring. True hope transcends circumstance and is the essence of faith.

Heart to heart with God

❑ Write petition prayers that share with God one hope for creation, one hope for your congregation, and one hope for your own life. Pray these prayers together and then exchange them. Offer to pray one of your partner's prayers for him/her this week. *Song: Open My Eyes*

3. Preaching for Reform

Enlarging our hearts

❑ Jeremiah 7:4 reminds us that even if we hear a statement repeated multiple times, it may not be true or it may not be fully in context. Build a tower of dominos, toothpicks, or matches on a shaky surface and another on a firm surface. Talk about the bedrock beliefs that support your hope. How solid can your life be if your hope has a shaky foundation?

❑ Jeremiah 7:5-7 tells us that we will be judged not by how the wealthy in our culture live but by the plight of the non-citizens, orphans and widows, and innocent individuals. Make a collage of pictures/headlines from newspapers or magazines that shows the lives of these groups in our culture. What do you see in or learn from these images?

burned churches
floods / hurricanes Thurs of Comp.

❑ Jeremiah 7:12-15 draws on the image of a recent disaster among the people. Make a collage of pictures of recent disasters. Talk about where your denominational relief fund has made a difference in times of disasters. How can we respond to disaster? Share stories of surviving natural/war disasters if you have had those experiences.

❑ Jeremiah 7:26 uses the image of stiff-necked people. Take turns keeping your neck totally stiff and trying to see what is happening in the room. What does that image indicate about our ability to see God's hope and future for us? What do we miss when we have a stiff-necked spiritual posture?

Nov April

❑ Chapter 7 of Jeremiah begins with a description of hearing good news in a worship setting. Settle back and remember the last six months of worship experiences in your congregation. Take turns relating the "best news" you heard in church during that period of time.

Heart to heart with God

❑ Using a map or a globe, take turns placing your hand on parts of the world that do not currently enjoy a sense of security— where peace is not a reality for a majority of the population. Pray as a group for these communities of God's people.

4. Covenant Talk

Enlarging our hearts

❑ Jeremiah 11:8 talks about the stubborn and evil hearts of the people. The image of heart repeats again and again in this book of the Bible. Using a concordance, look up all the times the word *heart* is found in Jeremiah. What do you learn about Jeremiah's understanding of heart and how he uses that image?

❑ God says through Jeremiah (Jer. 11) that the people have abandoned their part of the covenant made with God. The image of a God that will no longer listen to the cries of the people is a harsh one. Remember a time when God seemed distant—you don't have to share these times unless you truly desire to do so. Discuss: At the time when God seemed distant, who did you believe initiated the distance? How do you close the distance when you feel far from God?

2. Chapter 11 portrays a wrathful, angry God who burns his own tree—the people. God is seen as one who is setting fire to the people because they have set fire to other gods. What images do people in your group carry to portray God's wrath? Draw pictures or symbols of what the anger of God is like. You might choose to write phrases about what God's anger is like using contemporary images. For instance, one friend of mine says God's anger is like a laser that burns to heal. How does your group respond to the idea/image of an angry God?

[handwritten right margin: Does this bother you?]

3. Jeremiah 12 raises the question of why the wicked prosper. Tell each other stories of righteous people who have suffered and seemingly wicked people who have prospered. How do you make sense of this? If evil coming into our lives is not dependent upon our good belief and good behavior, then why live in covenant with God? *[handwritten: How do you prepare for tough times?]*

4. In Jeremiah 12:5 God asks how we will stand in the faith in a place where we are threatened, if we cannot stand in faith where we feel safe. Share with each other the places where you feel safe and unsafe to practice your faith.

Heart to heart with God

❑ Knowing that the will of God is a mystery to us, and given the angry God portrayed in today's text, it might be well to practice a resting-in-the-presence prayer with God during this session. Given that the reward for covenant stated in Chapter 11 is a land flowing with milk and honey, imagine yourselves in the most beautiful and peaceful and abundant place you can summon. Rest in that place of prayer; go there with God

Prayer is an invitation to God to intervene in our lives, to let his will prevail in our affairs —

for ten to fifteen minutes in silence or with soft music playing. In resting with God, we do not ask for explanations. We simply accept God's presence.

5. God's Answer to Prayer

Enlarging our hearts

Water is essential for life. Jeremiah 14 uses the image of a drought for the spiritual dryness of the people. Allow two pieces of celery to sit out for half a day and become limp. Place one stalk half submerged in a glass of water tinged with food coloring, and leave the other stalk without water. See how the celery changes. What analogy can you make when you look at this? How does living water of the Spirit enter your life? What changes in your life when you live "in the spirit"?

Jeremiah 14:11ff examines the problem of false prophecy. We are tempted to hear only the news we want to hear. Share stories of when people told you news you did not want to hear. How did you feel about the bearer of the news? How do you tell people things they do not want to hear? Tell stories about when you had to be the one to deliver bad news. How did it feel?

Jeremiah 15:18 talks about God as a "deceitful brook." Living in Arizona, I understand this image! Sometimes there is a raging torrent through the washes, and other times the washes are empty beds. The text raises the dilemma that sometimes God feels very present in our lives and other times God feels absent. Using the image of the creek bed, draw pictures or use watercolors to portray how much water/spirit is flowing through life these days. If your spirit feels dry, draw a creek bed in browns with rocks. If you feel a flood of blessing in your life, draw that. Share the pictures and the feelings they provoke.

Divine prayers — the mulberry tree (Abraham)? With time + patience, a rich grows.

Important to utter worthy words. Are there times when you feel unappreciated?

❑ Jeremiah 15:19 reminds us of the power of the spoken word for healing. Take turns standing in the middle of your group while each one tells how they see God working through you at this time in your life. Utter what is precious to each other and become the mouth of God for one another.

❑ Make tea together. Someone once said that "people are like tea bags. You find out what they are made of when they are in hot water." Jeremiah and his people are in hot water. While drinking your tea, tell about a time when you were in hot water and what you discovered about yourself and about God.

Heart to heart with God

❑ As you listen to a recording of the sound of running water or soft, flowing music, do the following exercise silently. Use two water containers, one full and one empty. Using self-stick notes or slips of paper with tape, write down situations in which you have seen God's presence and situations where you have felt God's absence. Write one per slip, using as many as you wish. Attach the slips of God's presence to the full container and the slips noting a feeling of God's absence to the empty container. Then pour the water from the full container into the empty container, and imagine what the situations of emptiness would feel/look like if God suddenly flooded into them—like water through a dry creek bed. Close by praying for the flooding to occur and for patience to endure the wait.

think about times

6. The Cost of Repentance

Enlarging our hearts

❑ Jeremiah 18 uses the image of a potter and clay. Craft an image from clay that represents your current relationship with God. After talking about your image, rework the clay and create a shape that represents a time when you felt very close to God. Discuss these images. Rework the clay again into an image of when you felt distant from God. Rework the clay again into a shape that represents the relationship you most desire to have with God. One final time, rework the clay into a sculpture that uses the clay of the whole group in some way. Allow this to dry and become a focal point for your group's worship center.

❏ Jeremiah is persecuted for proclaiming the visions from God that are his. Share stories about times you believe you have been hurt for proclaiming your faith in a public or private way. Did you learn anything new about yourself when this happened?

❏ Jeremiah breaks a pot as a symbolic act in chapter 19 of the text. Break an inexpensive or old piece of pottery or a mug, being careful not to injure anyone. Talk about the feelings in the group when they see something being broken or destroyed. What is God trying to tell Jeremiah's listeners and us about covenant by using such a shocking and seemingly wasteful action?

❏ According to Jeremiah 20, Jeremiah feels like a fool for speaking out, but he cannot help himself. The clown/fool has been an image for God's messengers for many centuries. If you can find a copy of a film from the 1960s entitled *The Parable*, show it to your group. (Check with EcuFilm in Nashville or a local ecumenical film library.) This film illustrates the foolish wisdom of God's word.

   Another way to experience the clown/fool image is to make each other up as clowns, using face paints and religious symbols. Or you might paint symbols on your face that portray your particular gifts in teaching God's wisdom and truth.

❏ Laments are statements of despair that exist within, not outside, a context of faith. We pray our laments in order to be honest with God and ourselves. In Jeremiah 20 Jeremiah laments about his role as a prophet who is ignored in his time. Would you like to write a lament about your frustrations because you are not being heard when you speak the good news of faith? If you have laments, share them and be attentive to the emotions they evoke. Share with each other your responses to the laments.

Heart to heart with God

❑ On a large piece of paper take turns, in silence, writing the names of prophets who were either martyred or persecuted for their faith and the places where they prophesied. In crossword puzzle format, connect the names of the prophets and the places where they spoke, showing the interconnections of the community of prophets through time. After you have created this art piece, simply look at it for a few moments. Then place it in the middle of your group, hold hands, and pray for the people listed. Pray also for those whose witness was never made famous and public but who may have sacrificed life and reputation for God's messages of reconciliation, hope, and justice.

7. True or False Prophets

Enlarging our hearts

❑ Jeremiah reminds us of the reality that not all who say they speak for God can be trusted. When have you trusted in the word of an "expert," only to find they were wrong after all. How can you translate that experience into this text? How do you choose who speaks for God in your life? Share stories about times others have been God's voice for you. How do you discern when a prophetic word is true or false in your own life?

❑ In Jeremiah 27, the prophet again uses symbolic action to make a point. By dressing himself as an exiled slave wearing a yoke, Jeremiah points to the spiritual state of his people. As a group, list the factors in our own society that enslave people, such as materialism, classism, racism, sexism. What other factors enslave and limit us all?

❑ In chapter 28 Hananiah speaks good news about restoration to the people of the old order from before the exile. Yet, Jeremiah declares it untrue. Picture the conflict between Jeremiah and Hananiah. List characteristics of each prophet that are attractive and unattractive to the listeners in the story and to you. Can you guess who would seem most appealing? Discuss a current event in the news where public figures are predicting different futures or outcomes. How do you decide who to listen to in that debate? Don't debate the issue. Instead, discuss the process of listening to divergent views.

❑ Since the Watergate scandal of the Nixon administration, the sense of trust in public officials and religious leaders has eroded. Discuss people in public or religious life whom group members hold up as heroes, and indicate why the public figure mentioned serves as a hero/mentor for you.

❑ Play a game of "I doubt it." On a piece of paper, write down three truths and one lie about a common topic (for example, your congregation, your city, your own life). Try to make your lies as convincing and appealing as possible. After you make your list, mix up everyone's papers and select one that is not your own. The object of the game is to pick out the lies on the paper you have. To debrief this exercise, explain how you sorted the facts to find the lie—the sorting process of discerning truth is the point.

Heart to heart with God

❑ I once read a proverb that says, "Muddy water, let stand, becomes clear." We experience this in our lives as we shift through the many voices and experiences of each. Fill a clear container with water. Mix in some material that will eventually sift down. Shake up the contents and invite the group to watch the heavy particles sort themselves to the bottom. Enjoy a time of prayer together, asking for God to help you be patient as your life settles and God's true word becomes clear to you.

8. Witnessing to God's Word

Enlarging our hearts

❑ Jeremiah sends Baruch with the words of God to the people. Write a letter to people in a place where you cannot go physically because of distance or access. Send the message that is on your heart. Share letters with the group. As you listen to the messages, offer insight into how each message could be made more clear. If you care to, tell others why your message was on your heart.

❑ Who in your community speaks for the orphans, widows, and homeless? How do they speak to power? Can you help this message be communicated? Call a group in your community that advocates for people without voice in the political process. Learn about how they speak truth to power.

❑ The church around the world has experienced times of persecution when the good news was silenced for a short time. Call your pastor or denominational office and learn about the partners in mission that you support through congregational giving. Find a way to send a message via e-mail, fax, or U.S. mail to encourage a mission person of your denomination who speaks God's truth in a dangerous situation.

❑ Learn about the tradition of civil disobedience by members of your own denominational group. Are there members of your denomination in prison somewhere in the world for their religious convictions? Find a way to be present with that person in prayer or by sending word of your concern for them.

attendance
new members
child care worker
chair growing
recognition of members
not
yet
grad

Make a scroll from a long sheet of paper and two dowels. Write on it your understanding of what God is doing in your congregation. Take turns dictating while another writes. Then have one person read the scroll aloud. If you are at your church, go to the sanctuary for this. Give the scroll to your pastor/ pastors with an explanation of how you came to write these things down.

Heart to heart with God

❑ Pray for people around the world who have been imprisoned for their religious beliefs. Light candles and name those you may know about. Turn out the lights and watch the candles. The brave souls these candles represent change the world by their courage. The reflected light of God's spirit brings light to all of us. Repeat their names over and over while listening to instrumental music.

9. Instilling Hope

Enlarging our hearts

❑ According to chapter 32, Jeremiah buys a field in an occupied land. This is an ultimate sign of hope in a day that is not yet, when the land will be returned and God's justice will reign. Verses 39-41 describe the heartfelt relationship that God will have with the people in the day of restoration. Using the people in your group, create a body sculpture of what that relationship will look like. Take turns being the artist by asking the group members to take the positions that create your sculpture.

❑ Share stories of the most hopeful thing you have ever done. Or share stories of when you saw another person exhibit infectious hope.

❑ Depression is an illness that manifests itself with a feeling of utter hopelessness. If you have encountered this illness in yourself or loved ones, tell the story about how healing has happened or is in the process of happening. Talk about how you might support people in your congregation who are dealing with depression.

❑ When a person is depressed, there are certain thought patterns that exist and defeat the ability to hope. They are called by therapists depressogenic thought styles. Below are four examples of them. Do you hear language like this in your congregation, family, work setting, school? How can you counter depressogenic statements?

a. I tried that once, but it didn't work. It will never work.
b. I know what others are thinking about me/us, and I can't do anything about it.
c. All people who are that age think that way.
d. If I cannot do it perfectly, I will not try. What's the use of doing something imperfectly?

Try to formulate a truthful and hopeful answer to each of these statements.

❑ In what period of life have you had the least amount of hope? Who were the people that helped pull you through and became God's presence for you? Write a letter of gratitude to one such person, whether they are living or dead. Read the letters to each other. Explore ways that you can embody hope for each other.

Heart to heart with God

❑ Share hymns that bring you hope and sing them to each other. Also enter a ritual of hope. On note cards write one situation where you most need hope in your life today. With music playing quietly, pass these cards around to each other. Hold each card, cradle it, and pray for that person before passing the card on. Then place all the cards in the middle of the room and ask God's loving presence in each situation. If you wish, you can exchange the cards for one week to pray each day for the hope of one other person in your group.

10. Renewing Covenant

Enlarging our hearts

❑ Chapter 31 of Jeremiah is full of metaphors. Working as a
   group, make a list of them. Respond individually to which
   one speaks to you most deeply and why. Indicate a place in
   your life where that image/metaphor applies to you.

❑ Jeremiah 31:13 declares that God can turn our mourning into
   joy. Ultimately the exile has the possibility of teaching the
   people to trust in God as the one who holds their future. Tell
   of times when you knew clearly that God held your future—
   inviting you from mourning into joy.

❑ Jeremiah 31:15 relates a time when Ramah would not be comforted. God's love is a comfort in times of inconsolability. If
   your group feels comfortable doing so, take turns giving a
   group hug to each member in turn. Cradling is another way
   to show support and comfort. If your group is made up of
   seven or more people, as a group carefully lift one person at a
   time and gently rock them. Pay careful attention to the
   person's back and neck. This can be a very emotional experience and deeply religious as you know yourself literally held
   by God's love.

❑ Jeremiah 31:17 reads, "There is hope for your future." Stand
   in a single-file line. Have the first person in line turn to the
   second person and repeat the scripture, "There is hope for
   your future," while looking him/her in the eye. Then have
   person #1 repeat this process with person #3 in line, and then
   #4, and on down the line. After person #1 has spoken to person #3 and is moving down the line, person #2 then begins
   the process speaking to person #3 and then #4, etc. This process is called turning the line inside out. It is over when person #1 is again at the front of the line.

   If done properly each person will speak these words of
   hope to every other person in the line. As the line is turning

inside out, many people are speaking at the same time. This takes some of the potential embarrassment out of the process for the shy people in the group, as they are not the focus of the entire group. This exercise can be done with music in the background or in silence. You may choose to do this in the aisle of the sanctuary.

❑ Give each person in your group a heart-shaped object with their name on it. Jeremiah 31:20 talks about the yearning love of God. Pass the hearts around and have each person write or attach a message on the heart, expressing one hope they hold for that person after having come to know them in this covenant group. You might use paper and pens, clay with paint or glaze, wood with paint, glass with paint as a sun catcher, whatever suits your time and abilities. Simple is best.

Heart to heart with God
❑ If you have been making the large heart each week with words from the text/lesson, use it as a focus for your closing prayers. Conclude the week with each of you telling a short story about your favorite moment in this ten-session study. Give three reasons why you are thankful for that moment and offer thanks to God.

General Sharing and Prayer Resources

Forming a Covenant Group

Covenant Expectations
Covenant-making is significant throughout the biblical story. God made covenants with Noah, Abraham, and Moses. Jeremiah speaks about God making a covenant with the people, "written on the heart." In the New Testament, Jesus is identified as the mediator of the new covenant, and the early believers lived out of covenant relationships. Throughout history people have lived in covenant relationship with God and within community.

Christians today also covenant with God and make commitments to each other. Such covenants help believers live out their faith. God's empowerment comes to them as they gather in covenant communities to pray and study, share and receive, reflect and act.

People of the Covenant is a program that is anchored in this covenantal history of God's people. It is a network of covenantal relationships. Denominations, districts or regions, congregations, small groups, and individuals all make covenants. Covenant group members commit themselves to the mission statement, seeking to become more . . .

— biblically informed so they better understand the revelation of God;
— globally aware so they know themselves to be better connected with all of God's world;
— relationally sensitive to God, self, and others.

The Burlap Cross Symbol

The imperfections of the burlap cross, its rough texture and unrefined fabric, the interweaving of threads, the uniqueness of each strand, are elements that are present within the covenant group. The people in the groups are imperfect, unpolished, interrelated with each other, yet still unique beings.

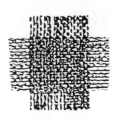 The shape that this collection of imperfect threads creates is the cross, symbolizing for all Christians the resurrection and presence of Christ our Savior. A covenant group is something akin to this burlap cross. It unites common, ordinary people and sends them out again in all directions to be in the world.

A Litany of Commitment

All: *We are a people of the covenant; out of our commitment to Christ, we seek to become:*

Group 1:   more biblically informed so we understand better God's revelation;

Group 2:   more globally aware so we know ourselves connected with all of God's people;

Group 1:   more relationally sensitive to God, self, and others.

All: *We are a people of the covenant; we promise:*

Group 2:   to seek ways of living out and sharing our faith;

Group 1:   to participate actively in congregational life;

Group 2:   to be open to the leading of the Spirit in our lives.

All: *We are a people of the covenant; we commit ourselves:*

Group 1:   to attend each group meeting, so far as possible;

Group 2:   to prepare through Bible study, prayer, and action;

Group 1:   to share thoughts and feelings, as appropriate;

Group 2:   to encourage each other on our faith journeys.

All: *We are a people of the covenant.*

Give me a clean heart

Give me a clean heart so I may serve thee. Lord, fix my heart so that I may be used by thee. For I'm not wor - thy of all these bless - ings. Give me a clean heart and I'll fol-low thee.

Text: Margaret J. Douroux
Music: Margaret J. Douroux; harm. Albert Denis Tessier

Have thine own way, Lord!

1 Have thine own way, Lord! Have thine own way!
2 Have thine own way, Lord! Have thine own way!
3 Have thine own way, Lord! Have thine own way!
4 Have thine own way, Lord! Have thine own way!

Thou art the pot - ter; I am the clay.
Search me and try me, Sav - ior to - day!
Wound-ed and wea - ry, help me I pray!
Hold o'er my be - ing ab - so - lute sway.

Mold me and make me af - ter thy will,
Wash me just now, Lord, wash me just now,
Pow - er, all pow - er, sure - ly is thine!
Fill with thy Spir - it till all shall see

while I am wait - ing, yield - ed and still.
as in thy pres - ence hum - bly I bow.
Touch me and heal me, Sav - ior di - vine!
Christ on - ly, al - ways, liv - ing in me!

Text: Adelaide A. Pollard, 1902
Music: George C. Stebbins, 1907

I was there to hear your borning cry

In unison

1 I was there to hear your born - ing cry, I'll be
3 When you heard the won - der of the Word I was
5 In the mid - dle a - ges of your life, not too
7 I was there to hear your born - ing cry, I'll be

there when you are old. I re - joiced the day you
there to cheer you on; you were raised to praise the
old, no long - er young, I'll be there to guide you
there when you are old. I re - joiced the day you

were bap - tized, to see your life un - fold.
liv - ing Lord, to whom you now be - long.
through the night, com - plete what I've be - gun.
were bap - tized, to see your life un - fold.

2 I was there when you were but a child, with a
4 If you find some - one to share your time and you
6 When the eve - ning gen - tly clos - es in and you

faith to suit you well; in a blaze of light you
join your hearts as one, I'll be there to make your
shut your wea - ry eyes, I'll be there as I have

wan - dered off to find where de - mons dwell.
vers - es rhyme from dusk till ris - ing sun.
al - ways been with just one more sur - prise.

Write these words in our hearts

Write these words in our hearts, we be - seech you, O God.

Text: Jeremiah 31:33
Music: Ancient Chant; adapt. John F. Wilson
Music ©1990 Hope Publishing Co., Carol Stream, IL 60188.
All rights reserved. Used by permission.

Other Covenant Bible Studies

1 Corinthians: The Community Struggles (Inhauser) $5.95
Abundant Living: Wellness from a Biblical Perspective
    (Rosenberger) $4.95
Biblical Imagery for God (Bucher) $5.95
Covenant People (Heckman/Gibble) $5.95
Daniel (Ramirez) $5.95
Ephesians: Reconciled in Christ (Ritchey Martin) $5.95
Esther (Roop) $5.95
The Gospel of Mark (Ramirez) $5.95
Hymns and Songs of the Bible (Parrott) $5.95
In the Beginning (Kuroiwa) $5.95
James: Faith in Action (Young) $5.95
Jonah: God's Global Reach (Bowser) $4.95
The Life of David (Fourman) $4.95
The Lord's Prayer (Rosenberger) $4.95
Love and Justice (O'Diam) $4.95
Many Cultures, One in Christ (Garber) $5.95
Mystery and Glory in John's Gospel (Fry) $5.95
Parables of Matthew (Davis) $5.95
Paul's Prison Letters (Bynum) $5.95
Presence and Power (Dell) $4.95
The Prophecy of Amos and Hosea (Bucher) $5.95
Psalms (Bowman) $4.95
Real Families: From Patriarchs to Prime Time (Dubble) $5.95
Revelation: Hope for the World in Troubled Times (Lowery) $5.95
Sermon on the Mount (Bowman) $4.95
A Spirituality of Compassion: Studies in Luke (Finney/Martin) .. $5.95
When God Calls (Jessup) $5.95
Wisdom (Bowman) $5.95

To place an order, call Brethren Press toll-free Monday through Friday,
8 A.M. to 4 P.M., at **800-441-3712**, or fax an order to **800-667-8188** twenty-
four hours a day. Shipping and handling will be added to each order. For
a full description of each title, ask for a free catalog of these and other
Brethren Press titles.

Visa and MasterCard accepted. Prices subject to change.

Brethren Press® • *faithQuest*® • 1451 Dundee Ave., Elgin, IL 60120-1694
800-441-3712 (orders) • 800-667-8188

Spirit of the Living God
Fall afresh on me.
Melt me, mold me
    Fill me use me.
Spirit of the living God
Fall afresh on me.

Jeremiah 33:3
(God's telephone #)

SRA Brent Shouse
3RD Herd
1St CCSQ
JTF-SH   APO AE 09308